Planning in Purple!
Your Week at a Peek Planner

Activinotes

DAILY JOURNALS, PLANNERS, NOTEBOOKS AND OTHER BLANK BOOKS

Monday	Tuesday	Wednesday	Thursday	Friday

Saturday	Sunday	Note

Things to remember

Contacts

Name	Number	Profile

People to meet

Things to remember for next week

Monday	Tuesday	Wednesday	Thursday	Friday

Saturday	Sunday	Note

Things to remember

Contacts

Name	Number	Profile

People to meet

Things to remember for next week

Monday	Tuesday	Wednesday	Thursday	Friday

Saturday	Sunday	Note

Things to remember

Contacts

Name	Number	Profile

People to meet

Things to remember for next week

Monday	Tuesday	Wednesday	Thursday	Friday

Saturday	Sunday	Note

Things to remember

Contacts

Name	Number	Profile

People to meet

Things to remember for next week

Monday	Tuesday	Wednesday	Thursday	Friday

Saturday	Sunday	Note

Things to remember

Contacts

Name	Number	Profile

People to meet

Things to remember for next week

Monday

Tuesday

Wednesday

Thursday

Friday

Saturday

Sunday

Note

Things to remember

Contacts

Name	Number	Profile

People to meet

Things to remember for next week

Monday

Tuesday

Wednesday

Thursday

Friday

Saturday

Sunday

Note

Things to remember

Contacts

Name	Number	Profile

People to meet

Things to remember for next week

Monday	Tuesday	Wednesday	Thursday	Friday

Saturday	Sunday	Note

Things to remember

Contacts

Name	Number	Profile

People to meet

Things to remember for next week

Monday	Tuesday	Wednesday	Thursday	Friday

Saturday	Sunday	Note

Things to remember

Contents

Name	Number	Profile

People to meet

Things to remember for next week

Monday	Tuesday	Wednesday	Thursday	Friday

Saturday	Sunday	Note

Things to remember

Contacts

Name	Number	Profile

People to meet

Things to remember for next week

Monday	Tuesday	Wednesday	Thursday	Friday

Saturday	Sunday	Note

Things to remember

Contacts

Name	Number	Profile

People to meet

Things to remember for next week

Monday	Tuesday	Wednesday	Thursday	Friday

Saturday	Sunday	Note

Things to remember

Contacts

Name	Number	Profile

People to meet

Things to remember for next week

Monday	Tuesday	Wednesday	Thursday	Friday

Saturday	Sunday	Note

Things to remember

Contacts

Name	Number	Profile

People to meet

Things to remember for next week

Monday   Tuesday   Wednesday   Thursday   Friday

Saturday   Sunday   Note

Things to remember

Contacts

Name	Number	Profile

People to meet

Things to remember for next week

Monday	Tuesday	Wednesday	Thursday	Friday

Saturday	Sunday	Note

Things to remember

Contacts

Name	Number	Profile

People to meet

Things to remember for next week

Monday	Tuesday	Wednesday	Thursday	Friday

Saturday	Sunday	Note

Things to remember

Contents

Name	Number	Profile

People to meet

Things to remember for next week

Monday	Tuesday	Wednesday	Thursday	Friday

Saturday	Sunday	Note

Things to remember

Contacts

Name	Number	Profile

People to meet

Things to remember for next week

Monday	Tuesday	Wednesday	Thursday	Friday

Saturday	Sunday	Note

Things to remember

Contacts

Name	Number	Profile

People to meet

Things to remember for next week

Monday

Tuesday

Wednesday

Thursday

Friday

Saturday

Sunday

Note

Things to remember

Contacts

Name	Number	Profile

People to meet

Things to remember for next week

Monday	Tuesday	Wednesday	Thursday	Friday

Saturday	Sunday	Note

Things to remember

Contacts

Name	Number	Profile

People to meet

Things to remember for next week

Monday	Tuesday	Wednesday	Thursday	Friday

Saturday	Sunday	Note

Things to remember

Contacts

Name	Number	Profile

People to meet

Things to remember for next week

Monday

Tuesday

Wednesday

Thursday

Friday

Saturday

Sunday

Note

Things to remember

Contacts

Name	Number	Profile

People to meet

Things to remember for next week

Monday	Tuesday	Wednesday	Thursday	Friday

Saturday	Sunday	Note

Things to remember

Contacts

Name	Number	Profile

People to meet

Things to remember for next week

Monday	Tuesday	Wednesday	Thursday	Friday

Saturday	Sunday	Note

Things to remember

Contacts

Name	Number	Profile

People to meet

Things to remember for next week

Monday	Tuesday	Wednesday	Thursday	Friday

Saturday	Sunday	Note

Things to remember

Contacts

Name	Number	Profile

People to meet

Things to remember for next week

Monday	Tuesday	Wednesday	Thursday	Friday

Saturday	Sunday	Note

Things to remember

Contacts

Name	Number	Profile

People to meet

Things to remember for next week

Monday	Tuesday	Wednesday	Thursday	Friday

Saturday	Sunday	Note

Things to remember

Contacts

Name	Number	Profile

People to meet

Things to remember for next week

Monday	Tuesday	Wednesday	Thursday	Friday

Saturday	Sunday	Note

Things to remember

Contacts

Name	Number	Profile

People to meet

Things to remember for next week

Monday

Tuesday

Wednesday

Thursday

Friday

Saturday

Sunday

Note

Things to remember

Contents

Name	Number	Profile

People to meet

Things to remember for next week

Monday

Tuesday

Wednesday

Thursday

Friday

Saturday

Sunday

Note

Things to remember

Contacts

Name	Number	Profile

People to meet

Things to remember for next week

Monday	Tuesday	Wednesday	Thursday	Friday

Saturday	Sunday	Note

Things to remember

Contacts

Name	Number	Profile

People to meet

Things to remember for next week

Monday	Tuesday	Wednesday	Thursday	Friday

Saturday	Sunday	Note

Things to remember

Contacts

Name	Number	Profile

People to meet

Things to remember for next week

Monday

Tuesday

Wednesday

Thursday

Friday

Saturday

Sunday

Note

Things to remember

Contacts

Name	Number	Profile

People to meet

Things to remember for next week

Monday	Tuesday	Wednesday	Thursday	Friday

Saturday	Sunday	Note

Things to remember

Contacts

Name	Number	Profile

People to meet

Things to remember for next week

Monday	Tuesday	Wednesday	Thursday	Friday

Saturday	Sunday	Note

Things to remember

Contacts

Name	Number	Profile

People to meet

Things to remember for next week

Monday	Tuesday	Wednesday	Thursday	Friday

Saturday	Sunday	Note

Things to remember

Contacts

Name	Number	Profile

People to meet

Things to remember for next week

Monday	Tuesday	Wednesday	Thursday	Friday

Saturday	Sunday	Note

Things to remember

Contacts

Name	Number	Profile

People to meet

Things to remember for next week

Monday	Tuesday	Wednesday	Thursday	Friday

Saturday	Sunday	Note

Things to remember

Contacts

Name	Number	Profile

People to meet

Things to remember for next week

Monday	Tuesday	Wednesday	Thursday	Friday

Saturday	Sunday	Note

Things to remember

Contacts

Name	Number	Profile

People to meet

Things to remember for next week

Monday | Tuesday | Wednesday | Thursday | Friday

Saturday | Sunday | Note

Things to remember

Contacts

Name	Number	Profile

People to meet

Things to remember for next week

Monday	Tuesday	Wednesday	Thursday	Friday

Saturday   Sunday   Note

Things to remember

Contacts

Name	Number	Profile

People to meet

Things to remember for next week

Monday

Tuesday

Wednesday

Thursday

Friday

Saturday

Sunday

Note

Things to remember

Contacts

Name	Number	Profile

People to meet

Things to remember for next week

Monday	Tuesday	Wednesday	Thursday	Friday

Saturday	Sunday	Note

Things to remember

Contacts

Name	Number	Profile

People to meet

Things to remember for next week

Monday

Tuesday

Wednesday

Thursday

Friday

Saturday

Sunday

Note

Things to remember

Contacts

Name	Number	Profile

People to meet

Things to remember for next week

Monday	Tuesday	Wednesday	Thursday	Friday

Saturday	Sunday	Note

Things to remember

Contacts

Name	Number	Profile

People to meet

Things to remember for next week

Monday	Tuesday	Wednesday	Thursday	Friday

Saturday	Sunday	Note

Things to remember

Contacts

Name	Number	Profile

People to meet

Things to remember for next week

Monday　　Tuesday　Wednesday　Thursday　Friday

Saturday　Sunday　　　　　　　Note

Things to remember

Contacts

Name	Number	Profile

People to meet

Things to remember for next week

Monday | Tuesday | Wednesday | Thursday | Friday

Saturday | Sunday | Note

Things to remember

Contacts

Name	Number	Profile

People to meet

Things to remember for next week

Monday

Tuesday

Wednesday

Thursday

Friday

Saturday

Sunday

Note

Things to remember

Contacts

Name	Number	Profile

People to meet

Things to remember for next week

Monday	Tuesday	Wednesday	Thursday	Friday

Saturday	Sunday	Note

Things to remember

Contacts

Name	Number	Profile

People to meet

Things to remember for next week

Monday	Tuesday	Wednesday	Thursday	Friday

Saturday	Sunday	Note

Things to remember

Contacts

Name	Number	Profile

People to meet

Things to remember for next week

Monday	Tuesday	Wednesday	Thursday	Friday

Saturday	Sunday	Note

Things to remember

www.ingramcontent.com/pod-product-compliance
Lightning Source LLC
Chambersburg PA
CBHW081336090426
42737CB00017B/3162